Muse

MARTIN REGAN DOVE

authorHOUSE®

AuthorHouse™
1663 Liberty Drive
Bloomington, IN 47403
www.authorhouse.com
Phone: 1 (800) 839-8640

Published by AuthorHouse 03/08/2017

ISBN: 978-1-5246-7531-8 (sc)
ISBN: 978-1-5246-7530-1 (e)

*Special thanks to Bubba Bradley for
the cover design. It is brilliant!*

*And again for Amanda; I am only alive when
the quill is in motion, you give me life.*

"Love will find a way through paths
where wolves fear to prey."

Lord Byron
(The Giaour)

Contents

A Letter from Amanda

Martin

Shakespeare wrote "How can my Muse want subject to invent,
While thou dost breathe, that pour'st into my verse
Thine own sweet argument"

You call me your Muse, Martin, I'm not sure how I inspire you, but I can say I am bloody glad I do. You have kept me entertained with your incredible stories and prose for several years now, which makes this a fabulously mutual partnership.

In a world where the written word is rapidly being eroded, slowly chewed and spat out in text-speak with pointless acronyms, the pure beauty and romance of yesteryear is reflected in your poetry. You may call me old fashioned, but I'll accept your soft articulate balladry over such charming modern gems as "I've got 99 problems but a bitch ain't one".

One should probably not question what makes a muse, for only Zeus knows for sure. So I will simply sit, read your ravishing words, and smile with absolute pride while joining the ranks of the many who have come before; who had the absolute pleasure of inspiring literature, the sciences, or the arts.

I really cannot properly articulate how honored I am to be your "Muse" Martin; I only know I am, and it is a wonderful feeling. As an old wolf once whispered across a page to me: "Teeth and Paw"

Amanda
Friday July 3rd, 2015
Bournemouth England

Foreword

Hello my friends, it is beyond lovely to be seeing you again (metaphorically of course). To those of you familiar with my work, welcome back, and to those of you reading my verse for the first time, thank you for finding the time to peruse my ruminations. Anyone who knows me well, knows my favorite thing in the world is to get hammered and write. Or rather, after the third or fourth scotch, I generally start frantically searching for a quill, because inside my head life has began to blaze, and it is a fire only words seem to temper. I have spent hours attempting to describe the moon. How it is framed by the sky, the various shades of light it seems to emit, the different shapes it assumes from one night to the other. So, it is probably a good thing my drug of choice is booze, because if it were LSD I would more than likely be in the loony bin by now.

I suppose this book starts, where the last one left off. In *From December to July, The Amanda File*, the book was in two parts. The first, being things I wrote specifically for my friend in England, Amanda. And the second half, a collection of pieces I had written over a very long period of time. This small book is all poetry I wrote specifically for Amanda in an eighteen month stretch.

To put a frame around my state of mind while writing this, I must tell you this collection of thoughts was reflective of my mood after moving from New York City to Nashville Tennessee. For those of you who have not spent a decade of your life in Manhattan, it is difficult to describe the emotions around leaving that City. New York City is an organism all to itself. It is a vibrant and exciting place to call home, and twenty four hours a day it thrums and hums with a life of its own. Whether you are in your bed or walking down Park Avenue, you are constantly aware you are in New York City. And its frenetic energy rises out of the pavement, and the sidewalks to massage your very soul. I won't lie, while New York City is an amazing place to live, it will also make you callous, and perhaps jaded, to the extreme. You will see more people, and more weirdness, in a single afternoon on the corner of 34th and 8th, than you will all year practically anywhere else. It is an explosion of humanity, representing people from all corners of the earth. It is exciting and fearful, enthralling and cautionary. It is an education of in-your-face anthropology. I highly recommend it (just don't lose your compassion in all the hustle and bustle).

Anyway, I left the bright lights and yellow brick road, to reside closer to my family, and find a quieter place to pursue my writing. I won't say I hate it in Nashville, they have a Symphony and a Ballet Company, so it's not all bad. It is a small city which takes itself very seriously in calling itself a city. It is definitely a quaint little town surrounded by a beast of a freeway system, but to call it a city seems a stretch to me. Now I know this is going to tick off Nashvillians, but that is probably because they take themselves so seriously. It is a lovely little town with a very attractive down-town area with not one train to access it (that one doesn't count, you know who I'm talking to). I will call Nashville a city when they decide to join the 21st century and build a transit system, until then, it is a lovely place to park your horse while you whet your whistle at one of the many saloons on Broadway.

Now that I've killed any potential book sales in the state of Tennessee, let's see what I can salvage. One cannot in anyway compare Nashville to New York. In Nashville it is small and quiet, the people are very nice and helpful, and you never have to travel very far for some fried chicken. It is a very affordable place to live, and if you enjoy country music as much as I do, it is pretty fantastic. Do I miss New York City? Absolutely; Do I dislike Nashville? Not at all; it is a fine place to live. So if you live in Tennessee and are a fan of the art of poetry, by all means, please purchase a copy of one, or all three of my books (so far), and hopefully, enjoy.

Speaking of poetry, if you are reading this, you already know you are a citizen of a very small population of people who still find poetry to be important. Poetry goes all the way back to the Greeks, and probably the Persians. The Chinese had a love affair with poetry, and all civilizations in Time, had a reverence for the art. There are stone tablets surviving to this day with Epics carved upon them due to Ancient Greece. The form survived, and classics such as Dante's Divine Comedy and Virgil's Aeneid came to be. In India there was Ramayana and Mahabharata, in England John Milton penned Paradise Lost, and as time churned on, the art form shortened from its Epic beginnings to shorter more poignant offerings, from men and women who attempted to capture their times, in a rhythmic style imitating the classics, while creating a niche of their own.

I am hopelessly in love with the Victorians; George Gordon Byron in particular. I find Shelley to be amazing, while Kipling tends to make me shiver. Some of the Americans are pretty tremendous as well, Frost and Dickinson gave a voice to life that resonates to this day. Sandburg's post World War II voice is haunting, and Whitman could describe the world around him so vividly, you could smell the forest.

Please understand, I am in no way comparing myself to these literary geniuses. I'm but a humble scribbler who clings to the quill, attempting to describe the world I live in, and the emotions all of humanity share. I have been unbelievably fortunate in finding a Muse in my friend Amanda. She has, over the years, been truly inspiring. So much so, this is the second book she has inspired. It was said Erato, the muse of romantic poetry, was daughter to Zeus, and one of the nine muses of Apollo. I can only respect her for the shadowy image she remains in the mists of time, but in this time now, in the flesh is Amanda Baverstock of Bournemouth England and I can say: she is my MUSE.

Martin Regan Dove
June 16, 2015
Nashville Tennessee

Muse

In this age we live in, where modern conveniences are taken for granted, where people have lived lifetimes depending upon electricity, tap water, refrigerators, and indoor plumbing…it is easy to forget all of these things are relatively new within the tapestry of human existence.

It was not so long ago, the dark of night was an entity to be feared, and had been for centuries. There was a time the night was not so much a place to rest, but where fear came to visit, and sleep was a fitful waiting for the sun to awake a new day. This was when the cloak of darkness gave birth to all the superstitions, to all the demons; which would plague man, when the sun went down.

This was before gunpowder. This was before the very ideas of freedom and democracy were born. This was a time of brutal existence…to our modern minds.

I am speaking of the Hellenistic period, because all philosophical thought, all ideas of law and justice sprung from their sandaled and be-robed idealism.

The time before Judaism, when there were many Gods worshiped and fawned over. Some considered great, others to be feared. But all as real to the populace of the day, as the marble statues left standing now, we gaze at, considering the past a faraway place we may never visit.

The word Muse comes from this period. Without going into too much detail; the mother of the nine muses name was Mnemosyne; the personification of memory. She slept with the God Zeus for nine consecutive nights, giving birth to the nine muses. Each of whom represented a portion of the arts and sciences. Of these nine muses, two of them, Calliope and Erato, were the standard bearers of poetry. One represented the Epics, and the other, the Lyrical.

I realize in this age of television and monotheism, it is difficult to imagine a time when Gods, Goddesses, and Muses were of any moment to the lives of us mere mortals, but I promise you...there was a time. And I believe to my very bones; it possessed a wonder and magnificence impossible to emulate in ours.

And now having proven I paid attention in at least one class (in the poor history of my academics), I should probably come to the point before you choose between stifling a yawn and doing something else.

I have no idea where poetry comes from.

I choose to think it is a Muse. Because there are no other choices I am aware of. There has to be some inspiration to gather the quills and ink, then apply them to parchment in thought. Over the years I have felt the inspiration to write. Sometimes it's just because a wayward breeze made me feel a certain way, but sometimes a muse comes along, and the quill grows a life of its own. As this is my second book in as many years due to such a muse, I think there is a magic.

I will never know for certain, but I will for certain; be happy Zeus and Mnemosyne spent two of their nine nights of passion, creating muses who felt poetry was important enough to be birthed by deities.

It's either that or scotch. Thanks for reading my book.

New York for Amanda

Through the open bedroom window are noises.
A bus stopping, engine idling, doors opening.
The various beeps, and whooshes of urban machines,
Mixed with voices, filled with their own drama lifting in
the air,
Another night in Harlem, as I sit and drink with the cat;

Loud Rap music, coming from a car stopped at the light,
Filtering through my window tonight,
The engine revs, and the music fades away
To be replaced with the straining engine of a truck going
up the hill,
Of Amsterdam Avenue from 125th Street

I'm sitting here having a pint, considering a smoke,
In the momentary quiet, coming through the window;
It is not often, silence in my bedroom I hear,
For New York City is right outside of my window,
And her sounds are loud, and always near.

The cat is curled up on the bed, as content as a cat
The horns, and sirens, and life sounds, coming through the
window,
Mean nothing to him. He is a part of that tapestry.
As unworried as sound, a mere piece of the light,
Illuminating this room, in this city, he reclines in life.

I'm listening to the radio. There is a Macy's commercial
on now,
Macy's biggest One Day Sale is coming
Don't forget,
I'm sure they don't do it often,
Rush down to 34th street and spend some money honey.

I stepped out of my chair, to smoke a cigarette at the window,
And the cat claimed my place.
I blew smoke into the night, listening to the sounds of the
wind
Blowing trash through the street, cups and papers and
human's refuse,
Tumbling in urban symphony; and let the cat have his stolen
peace;

But for a moment…and sat on him.
He left, casting me a guilty look. Not his guilt mind you,
But mine,
For reclaiming the chair,
The Cat holds many soft grudges.

I'll be leaving all of this very soon
The subway trains, where I am pressed closely into strangers,
While reading a book,
And hoping my bag is not robbed,
Typical days, I have become accustomed to.

This afternoon I sat by my window, a cup of coffee in hand
Watching the traffic, listening to the City,
Smoking a cigarette, and thinking not too much of anything.
A black plastic bag floated by on the wind, and I grabbed it,
Thinking to myself, "Well, I need something for cigarette
butts".

The cat seems asleep
Until I pat his head, and he acts as if,
He has been attacked, and licks his elbow,
And claws my hand,
Then bites and licks me; as if he does not know me.
Bloody Cat.

The buses are loud, the traffic is loud
Outside my window,
I'm only on the fourth floor,
Right over a bus stop,
A river of traffic drives by below me.

And I am sitting here thinking of you Amanda,
Here in New York City,
Getting ready to leave,
And go somewhere else, where I am sure,
I will still think of you, and send you verse.

As a Child

When I was a child,
In the long green grass, I would lay and look into the sky,
There were no troubles there.

Just clouds shaped like dragons and things
Castles, turtles, and sometimes worms;
The grass smelled just like grass, when stirred in the breeze,
As I lay, a child, watching a world he did not understand;
pass by.

I remember the pink webbing,
Between my fingers as I held my hands up to the sun,
And the great silence surrounding me, and in my head;
The innocent tides of childhood
Crashing gently upon the shores of my awareness,
When the only concern was a grumble in the belly,
A hunger easily sated, by simply telling Mom.

One year Dad bought, and gave to me a bow and arrow set.
A large bow, it was yellow fiber-glass, with a black handled
grip in the middle,
There was a quiver of blunted arrows, each one with feathers
adorning the end of the shaft.

I would lie in the long green grass gazing into the azure sky,
And fire an arrow into the blue,

Watch it sail into the sky, to slowly flip back; and come straight down,
At the very last moment, I would turn to my left or my right,
hearing the arrow thunk into the ground.

I would then pull it out of the dirt, the tip rich with loam,
Cleaning the warm soil from it with my fingers, smelling the earth;
To again fire it into the sky, reclining into its ascension,
Watching closely when it turned,
To begin the descent
Speeding as quicksilver, to impale my heart,
Rolling every time to the left or the right; missing its deadly flight.

When I was a child, it was this simple,
To lay in the long green grass, with my bow and arrows,
Firing into the sky; aiming only at myself.
Knowing the sky was firing back.

And the arrow, was nothing more than a game to be played, alone.
I realize now, a pierced heart in this life was the least of my worries,
I often wish turning to the left or the right…was still a savior.

In the long green grass; when I was a child.

For Eyes

I placed your picture next to the flowers.
So, as I recline into the evening, I may contemplate,
Two beauties, nature has chosen with which to grace my
eyes
And allow to resonate
Like a symphony for the sight.

Byron would have written I'm sure,
More eloquently,
And with a talent I do not possess.
Of beauty, and of flowers, of you,
What is love, what is felt, for he knew-

How looking into the night, at a face not there,
Inspires words to flow from quills
About the face floating as solidly
As the moon in the sky,
The one remembered from the heart, to reflect in the mind.

Shimmering moonlight upon the surface of a brook,
Insubstantial, but so very there
Floating it seems, on the surface,
Ethereally for a moment
A reminder, how soon it all becomes a memory,

Of your face, of flowers, of the time we were young.
When the moon, was never sad,

And brooks would flow forever;
When love was a fever, and not a scar,
When no one was old, and tears were only shed for strangers.

Ah Love,
Flowers, and pictures, and memories, and the reflections of
moons past,
Shimmering only in dim recollection,
Lighting forgotten candles like sighs,
Illuminating weary, but happy souls;

The laughter now, carrying the echo of, laughter then,
With a touch of "remember when?"
Plodding along we go, holding hands with Father Time,
Only it is: Our hands, bearing the wrinkles and creases,
Which Master Time seems immune.

And like a conductor frantically waving his wand,
Long after,
The orchestra has departed.
Encouraging the instruments still make music;
Do we hang on for dear life,
Listening for the music,
That fled with our youth.

I like your picture next to the flowers.
Because while I am far from old,
I no longer have that vim and vigor, what makes me truly young.
So, I gaze at beautiful flowers, and beautiful you, knowing;
With a great sigh; you are both only…for eyes.

In My Mind

It's only a voice in the air,
A thought inside the head, screaming for a way out;
The warm and, and warm touch,
Of your hand, the one I've never touched,
Touching my fingers,
And my fingers, closing around that thought.

The one dedicated to the idea of your hair, of your,
Your breath…
Upon,
The kiss un-tasted; the sigh
Given anyway,
I wrap into the web of my mind, while a voice screams "Yes!"

Music plays, creating a cradle of bliss,
And somewhere I am sure,
An ocean rolls with:
All the anger of storms and,
Calm of sighs;
And, a touch of us.

With an outstretched hand, and whiskey breath,
I ask you to dance.
The music allows desires unspoken,
And your smile, is a dress I would like to remove,
Kissing it away into a night, where the candles cast shadows,
Until it returns, to light the room

What is a kiss?
What is a caress?
What is?
That sigh… forcing one to recall?
Every day thoughts,
After it passes your lips?

The day is lit with a burning sun, but the night,
Burns with its own dark counterpart
Reaching, with a heavy step, to stomp out the hope
Of one dreaming, one reaching,
One hoping for the sun of another morning, and
This makes me think of you.

She said from across the ocean:
"The day here is grey, and the sky, is bruised and pregnant,
with rain.
And I am thinking of you sat writing
At your desk;
And I am smiling"

Love crosses oceans sometimes, and words cross like swords,
And we, we my darling, sigh for a second,
Knowing that sigh is only the breath
Crossing swords
In the night of our love, and now,
Is a part of every love, ever written in word.

Late Afternoon

The sky is gray, with only the hint of a storm,
Telegraphed, in what thoughts the sky might send
And a spring chill resides; in the grasp of the wind.

The leaves on the trees are drooping, and sodden
With the last rain; almost sad in countenance
Hanging off branches, as if guilty of new life,
Of being, yet again; the reminder winter is dead for a season.

It is a violent kiss. Spring spreading its wings,
A whiskey soaked embrace, promising a submissive delight,

Pressing you into the wall,
A calloused hand, leaving a run upon a maiden's stockings,
The harsh acrid smell, of a smoldering cigarette
Forgotten in an ashtray by the bed,
Whilst harsh desires turn into, sweat dampened bed sheets.

Time is the sky when she breathes, when she gasps, when she…
Becomes the elemental she, a She, she has always been.

I long for thunder to frame these thoughts!
Lightning to illuminate
This desire, this memory, this want;
Of a violent kiss in,
This afternoon of spring.

Sing to me lost Gods! Make me tremble in your thunder!
Like a man standing before the ocean a thousand years ago
Watching the sun be swallowed by the horizon
Wondering if:

He'll ever see its burning orb again,
If:
Tomorrow will never come,
If, dark clouds over waves is: the end.

And I sit here with this quill,
Poised, dripping ink; over the page unmarked
The cat curled in the other chair.

I, dreaming of violent kisses;
Of pressing her against a wall,
Her hands, clutching my back, through the fabric of my
shirt,
Fingernails digging, and sending brilliant tiny blurbs of
pain,
From my skin to my brain;

While spring is a silent storm…just outside the open door.

Rain

I'm sitting at my desk, a cigarette burning into the air,
The smoke curling up, and into the room around me,
Out the window it is raining.
The funny thing about the rain
Is,
You feel it, even when you are only hearing it.

We've all been caught in the rain,
When we were children, we gathered it about us,
Thinking it was only wet,
The sky, crying on our shirts,
We wore it like a badge, and smiled.

Time punishes childhood, because it takes it away,
And then the rain is no longer a badge
But an inconvenience upon the lapels;
Or the dress, Time has told us to wear
Stating rain is not friendly, but a duty to bear.

God! A child in a rain storm is fun!
They laugh at the sky, they giggle in the rain,
They don't care…how wet,
The sky makes them
They have no lapels, or dresses to break them.

I think it is an insult
To the sky, and the world,
That I own a camel hair jacket,
I hide from the rain,
When I'm pretty sure it would be just as nice, when wet.

There is a stream to this life
A creek running,
A river flowing,
An ocean, with a mind of its very own,
We should embrace.

I want always to look into the rain, with the eyes of a child,
Raindrops, running down my cheeks like,
Tears,
Always reminding me of; of…of well, hell,
When I was a child; when rain was rain, and there were no
years.

Spring Again

And again…it is spring.
I know because;
The softest breeze is reaching through the door
Like a caress, or an apology,
For the cruel touch of winter
To touch my skin, like a new lover,
And remind me, of the lovers of the past.

It is spring,
Bringing to life the multi-colored memories, of the ones before,
To dance in recollection,
To the music of new leaves turning green on old trees,
Like a kiss on the mouth,
One can't seem to forget,
But remembers often, with the tiniest regret

Like wine, cooling softly, in its stemmed glass
Awaiting lips it must, it must, it must
Touch,
Sooner rather than later, with love
Is Spring
Pressed grapes, fermented to become anew,
Making us feel for a moment, alive again.

The cat lounging, and stretching in his leisurely recline
Naps in this soft, and caressing breeze, this spring wind,
Feeling only what cats know,
Occasionally turning his head to slowly wink
In my direction,
His nonchalance, a reflection
In this mirror we call Spring.

And somewhere around the soft breeze
Beyond its current touch
Lurks summer;
Promising heat, the hot, a swelter under the golden sun,
Blending the sighs of those lamenting the heat to proclaim:
"Give me Winter"
The same voices, from its cold memory, begging for
sunshine...

For Amanda darling, it never changes,
People are forever and always the same,
We lose our reason, each change of the season
But,
My God darling, look:
It is spring again,
And we are discussing it again.

Love and Alexis

It is warm with or without you
And the wind blows the same,
Giving its chill, or soft brush across my face
The seasons change,
With or without you
Each memory of the one before
Not touching right away,
The new beginning, the new sensation
Because;
You, like the seasons
Will always be there,
For Love is:
Unchanging.

We speak of spring, as if it is brand new
And lament the winter
As if we've never experienced it before,
So much like love
If it is Love,
Will not be forgotten
Because, like the seasons
It may change with time, but never go away.

Summer becomes a hot lament,
When the grass is browned by the sun, and our skin
Turns red and we wish,
For fall again;

We desire always the next stage, the next comfort
The next platform, on which to sing again,
Because we think we are missing;

Love...
That ghost of a feeling, that ephemeral emotion,
Which is haunting, within, and throughout,
This path we call Life.

It is warm, with or without you.
Watching seasons glow, from one to the other,
And in each season, I miss you because,
Love is as changing as the seasons, but the same.

A single violin is a concerto,
Those strings, no matter how strummed,
Fill the air with their own season of feeling,
No matter the accompaniment, like Love.
There is only one. One violin; one season,
Which changes, but;
Always is the same...
I am warm, with or without you

It is the Love.
Doesn't change...

No Reason

A thought:

I had…

In a moment of flux, the beer and the scotch, greasing a platform to slip upon, for this:

Thought

My only regret is, she thought I didn't love her.
She went to sleep, wondering why we were no longer together,
Because we never talked about it,
And let it end on a sunny street in Manhattan,
Dealing tickets and a ring, and forgetting,
Why it had ever come to be in the first place.

We sat in French restaurants
We looked at each other over fresh flower arrangements
Smiling, as the world coalesced by in all its varied colors
Through windows we never noticed,
Except in the peripheral;
Because we were distracted by,
Each other.

We talked, yet never said,
What it was we were talking about,
And this led,
To walking hand in hand,
Through noisy streets bathed in lights, both day and night.

There was scotch and martinis,
A glass of wine in her delicate hand,
There was the Ballet.
There was a glass of beer while waiting for the bus,
While she still held a mask from the evening in her fingers,
It was Life.

The lights of New York City
The feel and echo of it beneath our feet,
The trains, the taxi cabs, the glow,
The hope and desire, and dare I say, love,
We shared on this stroll.

But there was anger too,
And misunderstanding,
And cancer
And not talking…
About the things that should have been,
The most important.

Life has the same ebb and roll as the ocean,
No matter how large the wave
The beach's sand stays the same, a ripple imprint lasting only,
Until the next wave
But
The sand remembers, for at least a moment,
The wave which was the stoutest;

Like a child's first memory of the ocean,
Salty, wet, and sand
Blinking the tears out of their eyes
Because an ocean will make you cry,
Not just for the salt, but for knowing the world is larger than you knew,

A Thought:

In this place, where there is no ocean to be seen,
While tomorrow you will be seen in an ocean,
I'm pouring another scotch,
And thinking of you.

Tonight

The cat sits in the cold, on the veranda,
His eyes a golden glow in the reflection of the moon,
A whisper in his gaze,
"You are thinking of her"

Music softly fills the air from,
The wooden radio upon the shelf,
Songs heard on a cold night, from yesterday's youth,
Playing now as, memories in the room

It is cold this March night, waiting for spring,
The air chill at my ankles, reaching up to my knees,
Threatening to touch my soul; this bloody cold

Time wears all the masques of the season's charades,
A summer wind, with the scent of flowers,
Swirls through the mind, on a cold night,
A blizzard in the past; reminds of a time seemingly worse,
but survived.

The music plays,
The pints are just as cold,
As they were when the air,
Was a warmer companion

I laugh into a sigh, in the inner silence surrounded by this
music,
And think of you.
Of British tinged whispers, followed by a smile,
There on my desk, is a picture of you.

Again, a second managed to become a minute,
A minute spread its wings,
An hour was born,
The hour a day, the day a month, the month a year;

And, there you are still,
My company in soul,
The beat of my heart,
While the cat watches, with cat patience, the time roll.

The spring is but a kiss away
Soon flowers will bloom before our eyes,
The cloaks shall find their closets,
And we will complain of heat and other things,

Because that is life; its changes are not even change,
It is but the breath before our eyes, on a frigid day,
And the sweat upon our brow when,
The wind becomes hot, and the chill a lost thought.

The cat just perched, to rest his paws upon my thigh,
His golden eyes filled with question,
He sniffed, and swished his tail as if to say:
"You're writing to her again, aren't you?"

I Think of You

There are those who say "The night is long"
But I do not think this is true.
I've lived so many years between the hours,
Sunset meets the twilight
That it is the Day, I think:

Is long.

Waiting for the peace of dark morning, to spread its wings in;
The silent caress of the night;

It is quiet, in this place,
Where troubles are at bay
Where wolves howl, and dogs bark nervously,
And the fox, settles into her den, dreaming of a full belly;
Is the night.

Now the cold hand of winter, strokes my forehead when I
walk,
Promising a chill, and promising death,
Should I not make friends with a fire,
Should I not make friends, with the desire,
To go on.

And in the cold morning, I scrape ice from the windscreen,
The car, engine purring,
My breath a plume in the darkness before my face,

Perched on the end of a thought
The warmth in a bitter cold,
I think of you.

In winter, thoughts turn to the pedestrian,
"Where is my scarf?"
"My feet are cold"
"These gloves are too short; this is madness!"
"This cloak is not warm enough! I think!" But,
I think of you;

And it abates.
The cold and the winter, the water-bottle has gone to a chill,
The grey sky, and barren trees, the wind
The bittersweet memory of a summer breeze abates because;
I think of you.

A British friend, in a time before, before time started
catching up,
Said to me once:
"Martin, where are the girls of summer?"
At the time I thought it was lament
But the British humour is deeper than that,
What he meant was, a celebration of warmth in the cold;

What he was saying was: "Martin, be sure to never forget:
A smile that moves you,
A voice which removes you,
From this winter;
And every winter"
Amanda, I think of you.

Each thought has an end,
Every end had a beginning,
The winter will not last
Spring will welcome summer, and then again the leaves
will turn
But all of that is of no moment as long as:
I think of you…

Harbours

(I spelled it this way specifically for you luv)

In a dark harbour, is where all the ships of dreams are tied;
Close to shore, but also close to escape.

Because all dreams truly of the sleeping kind, unfold in the
dark of night…

But sometimes,
The real brightness glows deeply, beyond, within and behind
Closed eyes.

We all board these ships of dreams,
Sometimes as cargo,
Sometimes as passengers
And in the best of these dreams:
We are the Captain, guiding our vessel to port.

We listen to those creaking ropes, holding us to the dock,
Whilst foreign voices promise peace for a moment of trade;

But that is all high thinking; an intellectual fault…
For the dreams, which matter the most,
Leave warmth against your skin, from the sun shining in
the night, within those nocturnal journeys,
Allowing you to wake, with the scent of grass still in your nose;
And a certain absence in your heart.

Beauty

I was looking at your picture,
(And thinking to myself)
What is it, makes someone beautiful?
Is it packaging?
What is it? Makes one sigh at the sight?
What is this thing Beauty?

I will be honest Amanda,
As I light this cigarette,
And pour another pint;
Contemplating what is beauty…
I look at this picture, and it is you.

Not because of the picture.
I feel your heart and it is,
Beautiful
I look at the picture, and your voice,
Fills my mind,
A lyricism as gorgeous as your heart.

And there is heat,
I feel it around the edges of my soul,
Contemplating you as a person,
Who lives and breathes and sighs,
On the same planet I stand,
And this heat is beauty.

It is not what one sees…
For sight will lie.
It is a feeling deep in where,
We are reluctant to admit…
It is the question, wreaks havoc in the heart,
But only to the broken pieces.

My God! Or Gods! Or what some deity created in wisdom,
This, Beauty?
This idea, separating the mundane, and crowning some as
beautiful?
Is the difference of sweat upon your brow from love,
Or from lack of,
The same love; beauty.

I gaze into your picture
Embracing this silence into my very soul,
In this silence is the tiniest of echoes proclaiming,
In a hushed whisper:
"Pay attention"
She is Beauty.

Because beauty, is not always the lie before your eyes,
Beauty is the heartbeat which skips
When you see or think of someone, or see something,
That means the whole of everything;
A mountain in the distance, where you used to live,
A voice you love embedded in memory, recalled in a dream,
beauty.

And there you are this morning darling
I hope with a cup of steaming tea,
Some Earl Grey, unadorned, to start the day;
Because I was attempting to define beauty with a word
or two,
With a drink and a smoke and a picture,
And all I could come up with...was you.

Summer

And she said:
"Summer,
Was not always my favorite season,
But now,
I look forward to the sun,
It bleaches the part of the soul
I would rather be blank"

She reaches for the warmth, the tan upon her skin,
Hiding winter thoughts, hiding the pale,
Pallor of spirit,
Of worries which surround her,
Wrapping her with,
More loss than gain
But summer is the season, when…

Blue skies like azure dreams, surround her head,
When she gazes into the sun,
Feeling its heat bake her skin,
And she loves.
She loves the sun, and she loves the heat,
She loves the summer,
She loves…

The Summer.
For it will not hurt her.
It is a season of sweat, feigning passion,

The air a heated hug enveloping her, promising one thing;
To stay for this season,
And hold her
Until the fall.

She loves

And summer is the infinite blue sky she gazes into,
Green eyes aglow,
Reflecting cottony clouds,
Into the iris, around her pupil,
Clouds in her eyes,
Reflecting summer,
Her favorite season.

She is summer,
But,
Love is of all seasons, and all seasons,
Are her.
She loves the summer,
The summer loves her,
I often wish,
I were her summer...

Because, it is now her favorite season.

I was Thinking

I was thinking,
And that's never a good thing, if,
The thinking skips time.

A flat stone skipping across the water;
FLING…skip, skip, skip, and sink.
Are thoughts like stones skipped across the creek of:

This life?
What were we thinking of?
When we were young and filled with everything but;
thought.

What was it?
That sinuous flesh of youthful thought conspiring?
To make us in the moment eternal, make us; God-like in
reflection now?

Oh that time…that time, was a warm water of a brook,
running over in the summer,
Caressing the skin of fingers dipped in the stream,
Which we flicked off, the droplets of water, into the abyss
memory would become.

I was thinking,
Yet again, how different the changes, the ones denied,
Have come, and are a more friendly embrace, than youthful
desire.

It is a lovely ride this carriage,
The horses of time, pulling us along while we gaze into
The wind; squinting our eyes, causing a slipstream of tears
upon the cheek;

Drying to be soon forgotten
The cheek, a place of good and bad memories, tear streaked;
And mostly forgotten.

Because: I was thinking.
Of all the good, and the bad, and the in-between, falling
like rain,
All around us, all the time, all the while... we are thinking.

Laughter passes from our lips, as relevant, and as dark as a
cry of sorrow,
I was thinking,
This is Love. This Life, this laughter, this...sigh, this idea
we all share;

It is a tear. One from loss...and one from a laugh, and one
because, why not?
Sliding down our cheek is what makes us alive;
I was thinking.

Blood

The world, in the moment, is a bit different now.
All of the burning desires, burn a little less,
And it is a gentler foot we place upon the path.

Hurt's less.

What were we doing? In youths embrace,
Blinded by the moment
The one we thought wouldn't change,
The one heated and immediate, the one; gone.

Angry love, and cold hate for ideas, or events, or exchanges,
Bit into our souls, shaping our bones, driving us to think:
It would never change, and we would be who we were,
forever.
Then, Time, stepping, stepped on us and then; we found,
forever is now.

The blood in your mouth from a good fight, or the blood
in the mouth of another,
Time makes prove, means nothing but, blood in some ones
mouth.
And the time goes by, asking your past to answer why,
Why blood meant anything at all, and why memory will
not lend forgiveness.

Where lay our hearts? That allow us to fight with one another?
What is the process of thoughts, make us hate to the point of killing?
Every war ends with men holding pens over paper sitting at tables,
Why can't they start with pens and tables?

This went from the wonder of time,
To the wonder of time, and the human heart; and I'm sorry
Not for the heart, but for the war of time, or the time of war...
For it seems being human it can only be blood, and war, and blood, in Time.

So now what, change? Change the whole of human history?
Say now: "No war! No aggression! No hatred! No differences!"
No way.
We are of a habit, and habits are difficult to sway, or stop.

The first addiction to be absorbed by the human animal was blood,
Not drugs, not alcohol, not love, not acceptance;
It was blood. And blood was delicious, so much so
The desire for it has never changed, stopped, or slowed.

Twelve thousand years, seven of them with writing;
And still blood.
The first pictures of humans were carved, depicting war,
Blood, five thousand years ago, blood flow of deaths lore;

Here we are, time behind us to explain, who knows? Maybe
a wrong?
Yet, death and war, better weapons and more...blood.
So the real addiction for the human condition is
Blood.

The blood of humanity powers humanity. There is no other
answer,
Every country, every race, every advancement is based upon,
Blood,
Humans greatest addiction, greatest desire, greatest will not
live without.

Twelve thousand years. Will we make it another twelve
thousand?
Does blood sustain blood until there is no more blood?
Or does blood run out?
We've screamed Peace for thousands of years, and stained it
with crimson for what?

To feed our humanity.
There will be no peace, there will be no respite. There will be no answer,
To the blood; but more blood, because humanity requires it,
We drip with it, we flow with it. We rip it and drain it upon the ground.

For the entirety of the human experience, we have only strived for:
The end of the human experience;
For every act of grace, there have been a thousand acts of bloodletting.
We love our blood, but not as much as we love, letting out our neighbor's blood.

So, now I'm getting older. And feeling kinder about life and its vagaries,
But I know, the Youth, blood boiling, even in their ideas of peace,
Will find new and exciting ways to feed their addiction, to kill and let;
Out the blood of whomever this generation exiles;

It is an addiction. Not new, been around for awhile,
But still, no matter the kind words,
Not going anywhere,
Time can tell, but some things never change; blood is the currency of human life.

For Amanda's Birthday

We are all victims...
Of Time.

It caresses us in youth, gentle upon our skin
Filling our thoughts with a nonsensical future,
It gives a sun,
Day after day
Rising, only to set,
Along with meaningless sighs, not yet filled with regret.

Time
It touches, it feels, it whispers its philosophies,
Softly into our ears...in the beginning;
Then like a river running ceaselessly beneath a bridge
It's whisper, the tiny voice in your head,
Becomes louder with having lived, and we begin to listen.

For now we have a past,
Something Youth cannot consider,
And the fences we've built and torn down,
Become as vivid in memory, as they ever were when there.
We taste our memories, like biting on fresh black berries
and bitter grapes,
Bitter and sweet, bittersweet, a laugh and a nod at...Time.

Every day we open our eyes and it often feels the same,
As everyday before,
Because it is so simple, so easy to forget
Everything.
When the road ahead starts to seem shorter than the road
behind;
We must take a deep breath and remember it is only: Time.

My God! We are but only humans!
We breathe and we love and we hate and we hope and
we cry!
We are the only animal balanced between,
Being an Angel;
Or a beast,
And Time is our master, whose shackles are subtlety.

A cruel yet giving master,
Who asks for nothing in return for the gifts,
He bestows,
Because he says:
"It is your choice, and your chance, from beginning to end,
To find love, to live like there is no end, until the end;
Time".
I send this birthday wish to you Amanda,
For I know you will understand
Time goes by, and is never ending,
But We; but We, embrace it in all its love and worry,

Because We… my Darling…know the secret; why its alright and always okay.
Life is our strength; and we love….Happy Birthday.

(Now I've had a chance to read this again for the book. Dear God! Amanda, I must have been in a mood. What I meant was: Happy Birthday Luv! Go have a drink)

Rambling Synopsis of Thought from the Quill

There's nothing written says I have to be genius every single time,
I reach into nothing and,
Just look for you.

Should genius rear its head, I for one allow it and exclaim:
"Amanda! These words are for you and,
Sometimes they rhyme (like a song, damnit!)"

And the time with the music blends into the night, and we…
Come together, here in this place,
Where dreams usually reside, but we reach as a storm; over an ocean;

To find us yet again,
Sitting, wondering if the words will come again,
And then, smiling to the air, yes, they are there.

We…darling we, can sit all the day long,
Pondering,
Reveling, because holy happen-stance! We are We!

Age makes us hurt, times we remember youth and its lack of,
Pain;
When we didn't take a pill, or a shot, or depend upon anything but our youth…

To give us the better part of the day,
Oh how I recall! A time a stolen kiss,
Made my eyes shimmer, not the memory, but the kiss.

What time is the time we call time and reside in time?
More than the past, where we thought time was stored,
Finding the truth is not time stored, but time unspent?

The truth I think, is the right now, the moment of this,
Where we embrace in time,
Embrace in the ether, the time which is now and forever.

You are ethereal,
A wisp of all I've ever thought to be good and perfect
Wrapping around my heart and soul, like Egyptian silk
from a forgotten past;

When silk was soft as skin, when silk spilt over the skin,
Like a soft wind,
And made you want to weep from its perfection.

Here I am, drunk as a lord,
Twisting verse for no other reason than the night,
Because thinking of you requires words, and smiles.

The night has a silence,
I looked around in this silence, at your pictures, and thought
to myself:
"Amanda would enjoy the quiet"

Coming Night

The air, is soft and warm,
And you can feel it,
Like a silk scarf sliding off,
Your skin,
A dog barks in the distance,
The trees, dark sentinels,
While above, the sky is a fading blue;
Covered here and there with clouds,
Spread out, as if to warm the cold spots;
Preparing for the Night.

It is still early enough,
To play the music too loudly;
But not so loud,
You can't hear the crickets,
Singing their own songs from,
Outside the open doors,
Singing of spring, and of summer, and of ancient things,
Only they remember,
In their DNA memories,
While the sky darkens into the night.

There is this moment, comes of the evening,
Right before the sky succumbs to the black,
When you gaze into the world above,
And know to your bones,
The sun is now far away

And experience the ancient twitch of worry,
Will it come back again?
Or will the world become,
The shadow outside a candle flame,
And night become forever?

Thousands of years of evolution,
Brought us to this moment;
Us wearing the adaptations and improvements,
Like a cloak
And still,
There lies with the hardiest soul,
The tiniest spark,
The slightest twinge,
Of fear:
For the coming night.

Now the sky is dark with;
A glow of clouds,
Muffled voices from an unseen corner,
A burst of laughter,
Then silence…
Of the sort makes its own sounds,
Softly.
The murmur of evening falling,
The sigh of a tired world preparing for sleep,
And the night arising.

The Night,
Where Angels and Demons, and Dreams all reside,
Together in the darkness,
Where Hope struggles with a blindness,
Provided by the black screen,
Of sleep and the evening;
When thoughts are both,
Happy and sad... and worries,
Niggle into all the cracks, the dark hides from the day,
In the coming night.

The stars can be seen now, sparkling,
Like tiny diamonds, scattered across black velvet.
A black velvet sky, full of diamonds for your dreams,
Tactile to the imagination
Light traveling from a dead and forgotten planet,
This light, only a memory
Flying through the vastness of space
To for a tiny moment,
Reflect in our eyes,
In the night.

I have in my hand, a very cold pint,
Which I tip towards the darkness covering the glass,
Of my windows,
I light a cigarette, and look for the cat
Who is asleep beneath the chair, not a care in the world.

I blow smoke into the air, watching it dissipate into nothing,
Disappear into the darkness;
And again, as usual, and is my custom,
Think of you in the,
Coming Night....

Seasons

My fingers are chilly, as I press them to my lips,
The sliding glass door is open to the night,
This April night,
That is cool to the touch,
Even the Cat is avoiding the balcony, his favorite perch.

Spring is here,
There are green leaves adorning branches
Blooming is soon to come, and an explosion of greenery,
To light up our senses, and our eyes,
For winter's grip has receded, and we may sing.

Here I sit drinking whiskey, into the night, in the chill,
Knowing, like every year, the heat will come,
The grass will green and turn brown under an,
Unforgiving sun,
And I will drink whiskey, lamenting the memory of winter.

The Greeks, Aesop in particular, was good at,
Prognosticating the changing of the human mood,
"It is far too cold", "It is far too hot"
We are an organism desiring the very thing we think we
do not have,
But still love in our complaining; the loss and gain of our
seasons.

What do I know? As I sit here drinking whiskey,
Thinking of loves lost, and loves gained,
The chill last fingertip of winter, imprinting my soul,
Again,
Knowing Spring will give me Summer as sure as the Fall.

Oh my God do I cry, and laugh and remember,
The whispers of a past not so far away,
And of a past farther than that,
The sweet taste of a chilled White in the summer,
The tang upon the tongue of a Red in Autumn.

And laughter. Each season has its own,
We laugh at winter in hopes we will survive it,
An echo in our cellular makeup, for those who did not;
We laugh at Spring, because we feel love again;
Each season is an emotion growing, as it passes once more,

Oh! And the Fall, the lovely, lovely Fall,
So many songs, so many loves entwined in its golden leaves,
When all the world holds a sigh,
Exhaling into a wind, becoming the wind itself, to caress
beauty,
The Fall, a crest of Winter to come.

My God do we live! Do we taste the wine!
We have learned to love, and lose, and gain, and re-grow;
The taste of honey-suckle, green is more than a colour-
When you press a blade of grass upon your tongue,
Tasting, and feeling, and being and more, is our galaxy.

We are seasons.
The seasons of the heart, of the soul, of this humanity;
The human heart listened to the world and gave us a reflection,
Orchestras emulating, and encompassing, the ocean crashing upon a beach,
And I sit here drinking whiskey, in another season...

Tired

How do you write "tired" upon a page?
Tired of spirit, tired of soul?
Tired, that consumes you.
How does one write that?

Can't read the Paper without eye-glasses,
Can't remember how to dream;
Can't seem to not be tired,
No matter how much sleep you have gleaned.

We were young,
And it was such a blue sky,
Filled with wonder and promise,
The back-ground screen to Youth.

I feel like I am dying.
I hope I'm wrong; I want a bit more time,

I'm tired.

I'm not sure what I should do,
I've been doing the same thing the whole time,
Who knew I was doing it wrong?
A Wolf never apologizes.

Tomorrow's not Monday

The cat is stretched languorously upon the planks of the balcony,
Gazing with feline indifference into the night,
Surrounded and enveloped in the symphony of southern insects singing:
Their own sonnambula; from the trees and grass and bush,
Darkness's lullaby…and the cat occasionally stretches his acknowledgement.

Tonight the moon has a pale yellow luminescence, lighting wisps of clouds,
With the tiniest of green hue,
Illuminated delicately, because of a deep blue/black panorama of Space,
The glow of the moon creating a filigree framing,
A picture for stars to dot themselves in, a painting for the mind;

And I think of your voice.
There is a lilt when you speak,
Makes me think of full moons, and the orchestra of nature,
A whisper in my ear of a thousand years;
Of remembering a resurrected forgotten.

We meet again.

Every fall the leaves depart from green to yellow,
Then become brown memories, floating to the ground.
To be embraced, and held, to give life to a new season;
After the snow, the cold….and it is only us humans call it;
Regret.

The moon is only so full because we see it as so,
It is the Moon,
And tonight, it is closer to the earth than usual,
Making it larger, in the human eye, than customary,
So we point and exclaim a beauty already there.

Except for Us

I think we have been here before.
I have heard your voice in a different time,
We have seen this moon in a past, smiling together
And like wolves never acquiescing to the idea of dismay,
Tomorrow is not Monday, because we are Always.

Our Days

Every day starts with the same light, in the eyes, out of the
night;
Right into the morning,
And every,
Tiny murder of the day before,
Clings for a moment
While we ready for the door.

Every foil of the past, the guilt of memory,
Faced in the morning, for a moment, cringing,
Before coffee, before the tea,
Before we remember
Trying to right it all, is easily forgotten.

The goodness we reach for necessitates,
An idea of ourselves
May not,
In our minds
Resonate.

But still, we must I think
Remember before and past,
How Good, was an idea,
We embraced
And hoped to last;

Our words they skip,
So often the life they feel
Using words against ourselves,
And tiny murders every day,
Becomes what we know.

I ask in our days,
To embrace these tiny murders,
Hold them closely to our chests
And make a solemn promise,
To keep them to ourselves...

The Heart is a Drum

A heart in the frigid cold is;
A heart…

And it beats in the spring as well as the winter,
When the sun lays upon the brow like an unseen spider
web creeps,
Warming but almost not there,
The heart beats.

It beats like a drum when you are afraid,
It beats the same when you're in love
And it beats to the rhythm of your soul,
Your breath, your wishes, your tears;

Does it beat…drumming and drumming and drumming,
You can feel it in your throat
Feel it in your chest,
Dream it even when you are awake.

Your very own orchestra is this drum-beat,
Certain voices make it strum,
Others, make it snare,
And some are a brush against the cymbals.

Oh! What music does this heart make?
And in every heart, in every chest, in every person in its wake;
How many times has your heart rolled?
How many times did it rest?

How many times has it sounded and felt like thunder?
Deep within your chest,
This drum,
This heart, the only one you possess.

Like a shadow in a summer sky,
The tiniest wisp of a gray cloud
A rumble in the distance,
The far away promise of a storm, a distant drum;

You feel in your throat as you look at the sky
Your heart beating like the echo of thunder,
Never wondering why, because,
The world is this heart, and you know you should smile into the heavens;

For the rat-a-tat-tat,
Pushing so gently from within your chest is only,
The drum beat of your heart beating,
To the rhythm of an echo, of all the hearts to have ever been a part of this orchestra we call us.

Empire of Lights

It was night, late, and dark,
Not dark like the home where I grew up, but still,
Dark in the way night is present.

The air was cool, and slipped over and around me,
While the engine between my legs screamed into the night,
Me a young man on a motorcycle, in California speeding towards,
No where.

To this day I don't recall if it was San Diego or LA,
The place I stopped.
But it was a curved bridge over a lined freeway,
And stopped, with the engine purring, I stood and took off my helmet.

The lights in the distance concentrated into the darkness expanding into,
Every castle I had ever imagined in a cloud, or my mind, lighting up the night,
Like Camelot remembered,
Like I imagine God's smile, when man does something right.

And I found, or realized; it is all an Empire of lights.
When I was young in the country, and in the night went to the store,
Driving through the dark, to just ahead in the distance a slow growing glow,
Of the lights; the brighter lights in front of me

Thinking how it has always been this way,
Man reaching for a light in the distance, until,
The light grows larger than the man ever imagined,
But then it is too late for him to reach back and embrace the darkness

The progress of light
Makes you afraid of the dim,
Because recalling your shadow has become an act
Avoided at all costs;

Is what you eventually see
Staring into its brightness, feeling nothing until,
Your bones sigh into the night,
It was only an Empire of lights…

This Moon Tonight

There are clouds, stretched across a yellow-orange moon
tonight,
Right up there in the dark sky
Just looking at me,
And while I write this,
The clouds dissipate like a diaphanous gown
Falling from a beautiful lady, inviting the night;

To make me think of a beautiful girl in England,
Who now this moment is sleeping,
Her blanket held lightly while grasping at dreams;
An ocean away I sit with a pint, thinking of her,
Wondering if the moon,
Is where she can see it, should she open her eyes right now.

I imagine her soft breathing, her sleep dreams seeing,
All the sleep thoughts, a day would rob from her,
Wondering if the moon shines,
Outside her house, a few short steps,
From the bed,
Whence so many dreams she has spun came to rest.

I write this for someone else,
Can you see?
Think, the ocean's dark reflection in the cast from a tiny
moon;
But not like,

The moon tonight,
Because this one is of you, you see?

And this is where,
Skipping lunch and drinking just enough that,
Smoking a bowl before dinner is a good idea.
Causing one to interrupt a perfectly good piece of prose,
Is I'm thinking,
A piss poor idea.

(I am either a fraud, a drunk or a dreamer...but I am exactly all of that with you)

Are You still Here?

The moon we talked about earlier, turned silver,
In front of, and behind a dark sky…

(don't drink and drive kids)

Seriously Love?
Still here?

Sub prime mortgages are only brilliant to the side of
thinking which inhibits any compassion for the poor (soon
to be poor-er)…

Weird, right?

You are my England. I am willing to bet there is no one else
on this planet, anywhere other than here, just me…thinking
"You are my England"
the fourteen hundreds gave you a (deservedly) bad reputation

But holy hell! It is England I sit thinking of, right here, when
darker clouds cover the trail of the moon…Amanda

*If you are still here…fucking- A Sis, we do rock! Like a round
stone, split down the middle, no matter how separated we
become, it is only us can embrace again.*

"The cheeks which spring from beauty's mould,
The lips which made me beauty's slave"
~Byron

…tap

-----To the Reader: When I wrote this to Amanda, the lines
following the piece were each upon their own page so she
might keep scrolling until the end. In my defense, if I may
quote Roger Waters when he was with Pink Floyd…"I was
really drunk at the time"

Sonnets for Amanda

What follows next are seven sonnets I wrote one night. I am a tremendous fan of the sonnets of Shakespeare, as a matter of fact; it was more than likely sonnets, which made me as a young man, fall in love with poetry.

A sonnet is so much more than a poem, because they are constrained within fourteen lines. They have a structure of their own, forcing the writer to be very aware of his or her ideas, as they quill the page. You have to know instinctively what it is you want to convey, and within the tiny architecture of fourteen sentences, pour your heart into the measuring cup.

A good sonnet is like a prayer. It is like a song, and it has a rhythm of its own. I do not think there is any other format in poetry more like dancing, than sonnets. They are intricate steps, each leading to the next, keeping to the beat of the music of your own heart. I wrote these sonnets in the winter, and I used a rose as my focal point.

I picked a red rose for Thee,
Today, while the sun was a cascade
Over my shoulders, defying the cold
Air of a late afternoon.
The stem was green and stiff,
And a thorn pierced my thumb
I pulled my hand back and watched,
A tiny drop of blood form, and drop
To the ground at my feet;
More crimson than the rose petals,
Adorning the flower,
Encouraging me to think,
This tiny pain I feel,
Is very similar to missing you.

I plucked a rose for Thee,
Because it reminded me of the colour of your hair
A thorn in protest,
Stabbed my finger causing,
A scarlet droplet of blood to form,
Then grow and slip
Falling to the soil at my feet,
I thought for an instant in hope,
Where this blood soaked into the ground
A blade of grass might grow,
Reaching fitfully towards the sky
Tiny enzymes unaware,
Their grasping reach to this infinite blue,
Is but a memory of me thinking of you.

I chose a rose for Thee,
Because they were there
And I was alone,
A single rose I picked
Brushing its fleshy soft petals,
Against my lips
Thinking of you in the midst,
Of the fragrance of a flower
Known only for its beauty,
But is often forgotten
While the scent of a rose is slight,
It is magnificent its tiny bouquet
In the senses,
Like Love, a rose is a complicated thing.

I picked a red rose for Thee,
I was in a shop and there were flowers
I looked at many,
Daisies made me think of you
Because daisies make me smile,
There were irises
But too blue for my mood,
Some daffodils called me
But wasn't quite my thought of you,
The carnations were funeral
The lilys a bit too formal
Orchids a bit too serious
And don't get me started on the tulips, so,
I picked a red rose for Thee.

I picked a rose for Thee,
I was negligent in my grasp
For upon my thumb a thorn made,
A tiny painful gash
I turned my hand holding the rose,
Watching a drop of blood line
Down the curve of my hand,
Into my palm
And for a moment,
The blood and the rose
Matched colors, and I knew,
Life is death, death is life, but we are
Beauty. Because we can pluck a rose,
And die a little for love.

I picked a rose for Thee,
For I wanted it to be spring
Winters grip is holding,
And the cold has become tiresome
I picked a rose for Thee,
Because it was bright and red and
For a moment, made me feel warm,
Inside
Where is usually reserved for,
You,
I picked a rose for Thee,
Had it wrapped in white paper
Surrounded by Queen Anne's lace because,
I picked a rose for Thee.

I picked a red rose for Thee,
The day had came to an end
I thought a rose for the evening,
Could give us a start
And make the day begin again,
I picked a rose for Thee
Because a rose would tell,
Though the day was long
This flower is fresh, longing for your approval,
As I longed for you, throughout the day
I picked a red rose for Thee,
Because Me, is a terribly lonely thing without,
You.
I picked a red rose for Thee.

The Single Word

There is a difference between worn and used;
Time
And not all kisses in the memory;
Shines
Bright lights often illuminate;
Regret,
But yet we smile into another day with;
Hope
Desiring the present to cover the past like;
Blankets
So the future might trod its own path to find;
Walks
When we are alone lost in thought with;
Fearing
Of mistakes visiting again to thwart our;
Soul.
Catching our breath, suppressing sighs;
Yet
Down this road of unwritten dreams;
Life
When sun and stars reflect in our eyes;
Will
Allow Times caress with both hammer and sigh, to;
Touch
What was hidden inside, this inside part only for;
You
To again in a mirror reflect a forgotten tear;
When

The promise was no tears more, but;
You
Reliving it all over again in;
Thought
A subtle lover is Time, but it is only;
Time
And every season we think we;
Forgot
Is but a season between me and;
You,
They change while we forget to look;
But
Blaze like the sun in past skies forgotten, yet we;
Know
A thousand lifetimes come and gone but there is;
Amanda
What is this thing time? This rolling thought;
I,
Think of, cascading over us, over me, but;
Love
It is the difference between being worn and used. What do…
You,
Think of this synapsis of thought in,
My
Mind? For there is no one worthy of the asking than the:
Muse.

Now Darling, read the single words as a sentence.

A Conversation

I love this romance,
It is like smoke drifting,
It is the reflection of fire in memory;
When wondering what the glow, in front of closed eye-lids,
Comes into question

It is hands held behind,
All who question,
How would they know?
We are light,
Shining in and out of the darkness...

I am no wordsmith,
No Shakespeare for you Muse,
Only a reflection of your thoughts,
You tell me;
Of a me,
I wish I could be.

So often we hold hands,
It is easy to forget,
The physical warmth of sensation,
Is not there but yet I,
Still feel your grip upon my fingers.

And truth were it truly true,
Would be no different or the same,
Than a phantom grip,
Left around the heart and in my,
In our, palms;

There is no explaining you Luv,
It would be akin to explaining,
The rain,
Or the heat of a sun,
Hidden by clouds in the sky

And Steve, your true love forever;
Is forever my hero
For while I adore you like the echo of,
Guns in the distance;
It is Steve

Who loves you like Time,
Falling from the clock,
Two types of love you,
Hold in your grasp,
Both a love immortal, both yours;

I can't imagine why you put up with me,
A drunk poet I am with nothing more than a quill and…
A drink
Professing his soul through a forgotten Victorian Art while,

You say I am,
The best of friendship,
Even,
Having never met,
While I protest yes, but

We've met a thousand times,
And each one, more magnificent than the,
Time before
Again we say in unison,
"Eternally Yours"

…and sigh into the wind.

Tap

Final Thoughts

There is a phrase: "It is better to light a candle than curse the darkness." I've researched its origins and have found only that is claimed to be an ancient Chinese proverb, although it also showed up in 1907, in a sermon by someone named W.L. Watkinson. Where ever it came from, I think it is apt, when describing writing in general, in this case, poetry in the specific.

I have spent many evenings in the darkness, with little but a drink and quill for company, speculating both the darkness and the candle, sometimes cursing the page for my lack of the right word. With windows open I have struggled to find the proper description of a symphony of insects crooning in the night. I have gazed at the moon wishing to use a phrase, much like painters have used a brush, to describe a wisp of cloud, dancing in the reflection of that wonderful globe. So many times a chill breeze from a winter evening has escaped my grasp, has touched me without my being able to describe to a world with only scribbles upon a page…what it truly feels like.

And this is where a Muse comes into play. For the writer, (or at least this one) a candle is a necessity not so much to overcome the darkness, but to provide a warm and loving light, creating enough glow upon the page, to structure ones thoughts. Amanda Baverstock is my candle. She has now for several years, been my reason for not cursing the darkness. She has been a light, a crutch at times, an ear when I needed a place to whisper. She quite accidentally became my Muse; and I will forever and again be grateful for her.

Right now I am listening to "It wasn't God who made honky-tonk angels", and Loretta Lynn is putting a heart into the words I am sure the writer did not imagine existed. That is what a Muse does. They add heart to the words, they on wings of angels, take what you say and make it fly.

While I have often over the years heard it said "Art is one percent inspiration, and ninety-nine percent perspiration" I feel this is both right and wrong. It is a case where for lack of this one percent, the ninety-nine, would be irrelevant, and it has been my experience, irrelevancy is anathema to cogent writing. Why do it, if it is not powerful?

I will never claim my scribbling is anything more than what words you read upon the page, it is my fondest wish though, that on some plain, where all the spirits of the past are known to dwell, Lord Byron raises a glass of red wine tipping it my way as if to say "Thanks for remembering, and keep trying".

Martin Regan Dove
Nashville, Tennessee
August 1, 2015

Printed in the United States
By Bookmasters